# LIFE ON TURBO
*Maximizing Your Life in 2011*

By
Travis C. Jennings

The Prophet's House Publishing is proud to introduce our latest volume of inspirational reading appropriately entitled Prophetic Pocket Notes (PPN). Prophetic Pocket Notes are the apostolic and prophetic teachings delivered each Sunday by the Harvest Tabernacle Church's very own Prophet Travis C. Jennings.

These powerful messages are designed to impact the lives of readers. They are guaranteed to make you laugh, make you cry, make you think, and most important make you MOVE!

Please enjoy the first edition of the new PPN line titled

### *LIFE ON TURBO!*

## Dedication

First, I want to thank the Lord Jesus Christ for this great revelation that causes one to be motivated to enter the ring and walk into their full champion status. To my lovely wife, Stephanie, my partner for life, you have always been the voice of encouragement, and the incubator for my dreams. To my precious children, Travis, Briona, Daja, Destiny and David Christopher, you have been the inspiration that has fueled me every step of the way. Most of all, I want to acknowledge that without this group of people this revelation would have never been birthed. To the church like no other, The Harvest Tabernacle Church, you have inspired me in ways that words cannot adequately describe. Because of the expectation and anticipation that you bring every week, you pulled this prophetic intrusive revelation out of me. I share the same sentiments with Apostle Paul when he said, "I cease not to make mention of you in my prayers."

LIFE ON TURBO. Copyright© 2010 by Travis C. Jennings. All rights reserved. Printed in the United States of America. No part of this book may be reproduced or transmitted in any form or by any means, electronic or mechanical, including photocopying, recording, or by any information storage and retrieval system, without written permission from the publisher.

> The Prophet's House Publishing
> 1450 S. Deshon Road, Lithonia, GA 30058.
> www.theharvesttabernacle.org

Scripture references taken from The Holy Bible: King James Version

"Scripture quotations taken from the New American Standard Bible®, Copyright © 1960, 1962, 1963, 1968, 1971, 1972, 1973, 1975, 1977, 1995 by The Lockman Foundation
Used by permission." (www.Lockman.org)

"Scripture taken from The Message. Copyright © 1993, 1994, 1995, 1996, 2000, 2001, 2002. Used by permission of NavPress Publishing Group."

ISBN: 978-0-615-27361-7

Printed in the Unites States of America

## LIFE ON TURBO
### *Maximizing Your Life*

The reason why you are still breathing is because there is destiny on your life. There is purpose on your life. The reason you did not have a break down is because there was purpose on your life. Not only the Holy Ghost, but also purpose kept you. Not only God, but also purpose kept you. All the mistakes you made, thank God for purpose!

I am talking about Life on Turbo!

> *The thief comes only to steal and kill and destroy; I came that they may have life, and have it abundantly.*
> *John 10:10 (NAS)*

Ephesians 5:16 speaks of redeeming the times because the days are evil. I believe in these last days, God has redeemed the time. The Lord spoke to me and said that there is an express lane reserved for the progressive, passionate, and prophetic believers. To be eligible to utilize the express lane, one must travel with at least one other person. I believe that this is the season for all of the dreams, potential plans, and the visions housed in us to manifest. I believe that this year we will begin to demonstrate our God-given purpose and reach the place called destiny. You will get there quicker than you would ever imagine. Are you ready? Let's enter the turbo lane!

*Romans 13:10-12 Love worketh no ill to his neighbour: therefore, love is the fulfilling of the law. And that, knowing the time, that now it is high time to awake out of sleep: for now is our salvation nearer than when we believed. The night is far spent, the day is at hand: let us therefore cast off the works of darkness, and let us put on the armour of light.*

The above scripture is not talking about being saved or coming into the Lord Jesus. It is talking about deliverance. Did you know that you could be saved, yet still need deliverance? There are two forms of deliverance: *spiritual* and *physical*.

Many people understand what spiritual deliverance is, but some of you may need physical deliverance. In other words, you need a physical manifestation of God's goodness in your physical world. An example of this could be in areas such as your finances. Your debt is high, and your income is low. Your credit is not where you want it to be. You can't even remember when you had a credit score above 600. God spoke to me and said, "Tell my people that this year they are getting ready to live life on turbo."

Romans and Ephesians show that everything is about redeeming the time. Now is high time, and because of this you can't get bothered by petty distractions, especially in the church.

I say this because, we can miss the move of God by distractions brought about by people, in particular, church people. Petty whining such as *'so and so didn't shake my hand,'* or *'she didn't give me a hug,'* or *'he cut his eyes at me'* are heard throughout many congregations across the nation.

Brothers and sisters, it's time to get over that. If they never speak to you again, love them in Jesus' name and keep it moving. You have too much anointing in you to let (your anointing) short circuit because they can't speak to you. In fact, love the hell out of them! It's time to move on. It's time to live life on turbo.

There are two kinds of people in the world today: people that wait for things to happen and people who make things happen. If you are going to reach your place in destiny, you are going to have to muster up enough strength to make things manifest in your life. God needs your permission and your participation to make something happen in your life.

## YOU ARE MORE THAN MEETS THE EYE

Many people in the church are asleep concerning the will of God. They don't even know who they are, let alone, the person sitting next to them. If they really had a revelation of who was sitting next to them, they would sow into your ministry. If they really discerned who was sitting next to them, they would discover that you are a champion. Tell them not to look at your battle scars, your clothes, or your shoes because you are more than meets the eye. You have more power packing on the inside of you than what they can see.

This isn't the time to put up with old issues and old hurts. You can't live your life in the past. You can't let yourself be paralyzed by what she said or what he said. God has invested a ministry in your spirit and you have to do what he has called you to do. You can't be bogged down with that foolishness any longer.

## MISJUDGED AND MISINTERPRETED

A lot of you have been misjudged and misinterpreted by people who don't even know you. Do not let the religious witches mess up your spirit. If you know that you have been living holy, praying, serving God, and not fornicating, you don't have jack to prove to them anymore.

Church folks are the main ones who get

bent out of shape over things that God created in you. It does not matter what you do or what you wear, they will find faults.

*If you wear black...they say, 'she's depressed'*
*If you wear white...they say, 'she thinks she's all holy now'*
*If you wear a dress...they say, 'she wants to be like First Lady because she always wears dresses.'*
*If you wear pants...they say, 'she's a ho. She knows she shouldn't be coming into God's house with pants on.'*
*If you wear blue...they say, 'she must have the blues.'*
*If you wear red...they say, 'she's a Jezebel!'*
*If you wear color in her hair...they say, 'she's too fast.*

With some of these people, you can't win for losing. I came to prophesy! Do not be dictated by church folks anymore. If you like it, and God said wear it, put it on! It is time to get out of the church and step into the kingdom.

## IT'S TIME TO MOVE ON

***John 10:10 states, 'the thief cometh not but for to steal, to kill and to destroy. I am come that they might have life and have it more abundantly'***

In this passage, the word *life* in the Greek means 'Zoe.' The Zoe life is the God kind of life. It is a life filled with power, authority and dominion. When people are living the God kind of life, they are exercising the God kind of faith. They possess the same authority that God used in Genesis when he declared, "let there be" and there was. When one is living the God kind of life, they can speak into chaos and confusion and cause things to manifest for the Glory of God. So don't allow fear, frustration and past failure to paralyze you. Keep it moving!

It feels real good to see a group of blood washed, blood bought people, who may still be going through pain, problems, pressure and perplexities, yet who have embraced the spirit of the kingdom. They have moved beyond yesterday's pain and their best days are ahead.

> **Now is the time to live the Zoë life, which Christ has made available for us to live freely.**

*Yeah, he lied on you...move on*
*Yeah, she talked about you...move on*
*Yeah, he left you with all your babies...move on*
*The dog bit you, and the cat scratched you...move on.*
*They laid you off brother. You had children to take care of, they didn't ask you or give you an explanation, they just said this is your last day...move on.*

These were folks that you put your hope in, your confidence in, and they let you down. Despite everything, we must move on beyond yesterday's pain and recognize that your best days are ahead.

## THE ENEMY BLACKMAILS WITH FEAR

The enemy has tried his best to blackmail your future. He knows that if you tap into who you really are, you would be a formidable force against the kingdom of darkness. Therefore, he tries to attack you with a spirit of fear. However, the fear we experience is not fear of failure, but of success. We are afraid of the genius God put inside of us. We are afraid of our potential. The bible says, *'greater is he that is in me, than he that is in the world.'*

You have a unique, distinct, one-of- a-kind genius on the inside of you. There is a combination to a special lock that only you know how to open. The enemy has been trying to keep our past in front of us to black mail our future through unmet needs, unresolved issues, and unhealed hurts.

He has been painting pictures and talking to your spirit telling you that you are evil. You can be in church dancing, singing, and giving God the praise, and the enemy will whisper in your ear, telling you to shut up, and calling you a hypocrite. You know you have been living holy, paying your tithes, giving your offering, giving God the glory, but the enemy is telling you to sit down.

You know you are not living two lives, but the enemy is putting thoughts in your mind that you are evil. The devil is a liar! You can't do anything when birds fly over your head, but you have the power to prevent them from nesting in your hair. In other words, the enemy will try you by conjuring up all types of images and faults, but you don't have to receive his messages. The bible says that we must cast down the imagination and every thought that comes against the knowledge of Jesus Christ. Regardless of the blackmail, give God a praise and move past yesterday's pain.

## MOVING PAST THE PAIN OF BAD RELATIONSHIPS

Shaquita thought Bernard was her Boaz. He got on one knee and proposed to her. He told her that God revealed that she was the one for him. Shortly after, and without notice, Shaquita found out Bernard was engaged to another girl in the church whom he eventually married! He was with Shaquita in '08, Tamika in '09, and now he's with Tonja in 2010. After Tonja, he's going to be with Brother Tyrone because he doesn't know what he wants nor who he wants. Bernard was not the man that God had for Shaquita, but because of her low self-esteem, she kept trying to make it work. Because she desired to be married, she ignored the warning signs in hopes that things would get better. Despite the embarrassment he may have caused, she had to move past yesterday's pain.

Darnell said, Lauryn promised him that she loved him. All she was trying to do was pay her cell phone bill. Sisters, if you want to maximize your life, you have to come out of that 'get over' spirit. Whenever you see a man, you see a dollar sign. When you see a man, you see your daddy. He's not your daddy! He's your husband! Your daddy was a mess; this is a man of God. Your daddy may have abused you, hurt you, and mistreated you. He is NOT your father and you cannot hold him hostage to what your daddy did. We harbor unmet needs, unresolved issues and unhealed hurts. If the needs go unmet, the hurts unhealed, and the issues unresolved, we will carry old baggage in a new place and space in our lives. You have to move past yesterday's pain.

I know this is a hard message to swallow,

but I am somebody who moved past yesterday's pain. My mother was a crack addict. She had me when she was 14 years old. All my life, people told me that I would be nothing. Despite their comments, I chose to do things differently. I am the only one in my family who had children in marriage because I said I would be the first one to have a marriage. I did not fornicate. I did not have babies out of wedlock. I cursed the curse. You have to curse the curses from your mother and father's side then move on because your best days are ahead.

My mother is no longer addicted to crack cocaine. In fact, she is now teaching others how to get free and stay free. Our relationship is one that exemplifies God's restoration plan. Now, what if I had unresolved issues with her, I would have never moved on to my best days, but, because I moved on to my best days, I became a better me. I reached back and pulled my mother with me, and now, our best days are ahead.

## THE ENEMY IS TRYING TO SILENCE YOUR DREAMS

The enemy has caused our dreams to be silent. Think of your conscience (that voice in your ear) as a personal GPS navigational system that dictates your decisions. The navigational system maps out directions for you. First, it calculates the route, and then it instructs you when to begin. If you make a wrong turn along the way, it will tell you to get back on track. When you get off the designated route, a warning tells you to get back on course.

> When you allow the enemy's voice to enlarge in your life, your navigation system gets quiet.

When you allow the enemy's voice to enlarge in your life, your navigation system gets quiet. As a result, you make wrong turn, after wrong turn, delaying your arrival and hindering your progress. The voice used to be loud, but now it is silent. Because you have ceased praying and stopped reading your word, and believing, it is not as active like it used to be.

Today the dreamer on the inside of you, with a parched throat, and crack in her voice speaks, and says, 'it has been painful to watch you settle for less. It has been painful to see you work on a job beneath your talents and capabilities, accepting the roles that others have assigned to you, and giving up the creativity to pursue that which fuels your ambition.'

Unfortunately, that is a reality for many people. Out of our need to please people, we accept the roles that others have assigned us not even considering our dreams or life purpose. Consider this scenario. You barely finished high school. Your parents were dropouts. You had a baby out of wedlock, so they say you are headed in the same direction; therefore, your life expectations should not be great. Statistically speaking, you are doomed. Because of this, others try to take control of your life. Mr. Employer sits back in his chair, peers at you over his glasses, and tells you that the job you applied for is no longer available. What he is going to *do* for you is place you in another position temporarily until your dream job comes available, yet the opportunity never comes. Have you ever had people do that to you? What was supposed to be a temporary

> God called you to millions, so do not settle for hundreds.

employment solution has turned into a permanent placement.

Oh, but the dreamer on the inside of you says that this is not the year to accept roles that others have assigned to you. You are not going to give up your creative pursuits to work beneath your talents and your capabilities--not in this season! God called you to millions, so do not settle for hundreds.

Today, the navigation system is speaking in your ear: "I'm the part of you that longs to be all that you were created to be." Remember back in the day when you had big plans, great ambition, and knew that there would be obstacles yet you pressed on. You were so passionate about your dream that you accepted the challenges. What happened? Where is your fight?

You may have had some pitfalls along your way to destiny. There may have been obstacles, and you pulled to the side of the road to take a water break, but in the midst of all of this, the Holy Ghost (your navigational system) has already considered your end. He already determined your destiny. Now get back on the designated route.

I do not care what your mama said or what your daddy did. I do not care what happened last year or last month. The Holy Ghost is telling me to tell you to GET BACK ON ROUTE! It is not too late. The devil does not want you to hear that. I believe God has something greater and something better in store for you.

## FORGETTING THOSE THINGS WHICH ARE BEHIND

If we are going to live life on turbo, you are going to have to forget the things that are behind. Rather than look at what lies ahead, you keep looking behind. For example, you may have an emotional spending problem that stemmed from your childhood because your family was poor. They could never save money. Now that you are an adult, you spend money to make up for what you lacked during your childhood.

You are spending money you don't even have, buying clothes you don't need, impressing people you don't even like. You are robbing Peter and Paul only to wear St. Johns. Yet, if God told you to give a $1000 in the offering, you would say you don't have it. Sister you're not fooling anyone. We know you don't have any money, looking funny. This is your word to come out of poverty!

By holding onto the past, we paralyze the present. One must gather up enough strength to shift from the past, shift into their now, and then shift into the future. You must believe that your future glory outweighs your present pain. Many people master the art of pleasing people and they never embrace the art of pleasing God. If one is to please the Lord, he must forget those things that are behind and reach forth onto those things, which are before. If one is to reach, they must begin to stretch. Sometimes the Lord will cause you to stretch in your money, in your marriage, and even in your ministry. Be assured that when

God stretches you, he is preparing you to propel further than you have ever imagined.

Brother, because all of your friends were promiscuous, you, do not want to live holy. You are so stuck on pleasing them that you do not even realize that if you begin to live for God, and give up sexual immoralities, then God will put money in your pocket so you won't have to put money in Pebbles' G-string. You must leave old playgrounds and old playmates alone.

## IT'S HIGH TIME FOR GOD'S PEOPLE TO SHIFT

Because of the state of the economy today, not only are companies and organizations suffering, but also the church. People are not giving their tithes and offering. It is interesting that the porn industry has not lost any money. Why is that? It is because people are going to continue to do what they want to do. It is not just the men either. Don't you know that 50% of the people addicted to porn are women? Don't get it twisted. There are a lot of nasty sisters out there who cannot get enough of the African King "Mandinko" of Chippendales.

## DETERMINE THE WORTH YOUR DREAM

Why hasn't the porn industry been affected by the economy? Let us investigate the life of the exotic dancer Pebbles. I'm going to tell you why Pebbles has more money than the women do in the church. First, Pebbles takes her job seriously. She is at work on Tuesday, Wednesday, Thursday, Friday, Saturday and even Sunday! She invests in her product. Everything is in place. She looks good, and she is not overweight. If she needs an increase, she does what it takes to invest in herself to sell her product. This may mean a gym membership, plastic surgery, or implants.

Surprisingly, Pebbles isn't sexually active. You've probably had more sex than she has. The reason why Pebbles has more money than the sanctified women is that she takes her career more seriously. The church sisters are always at church, singing, *'come by here my Lord, come by here'* while Pebbles is putting her faith in action and in the process, she's taking the Lord with her along with your husband's money.

I'm not just talking to the married women either, the single women are just as guilty. Some of you who fall into this category have no excuse. Instead of working your dream, you sit on your gifts and talents, moaning about wanting a husband. Pebbles understands that she does not need a husband to be successful. She is working it by herself. What have you done about the talent and the capabilities that God has put inside of you? I'm not talking about prophesying, now. You are lying if you say that the only thing you have is a prophetic gift. God is not stupid nor is he limited. He gives more than spiritual gifts. He will give you a talent so that you can work it in the earth realm so you can be a Kingdom financier.

This year, you will have to connect with the person who has your answer, and disconnect with the one who has your problems. You will have to connect with two words: commitment and success because commitment breeds success.

For instance, you started a new job and already you are taking days off. Why are you taking the day off when you don't have any money? Stop calling off! Stop taking sick days. They are getting ready to fire you, and you don't even know it! You need to get up an hour early every morning and seek the Lord in prayer and meditation so your day can be set and you can get to work 30 minutes earlier.

Your daily ambition should be to do your job better than your team leader and your supervisor. God is getting ready to make a divine switch, and if you apply yourself, you may be the one selected to take over his office because you will be ahead of the game.

Now back to Pebbles. Did you know Pebbles is prophetic? How so, you may ask.

Let's look at John and Will, two potential clients who've just entered the strip club. Pebbles scopes them both out from across the room. John looks like a nerd in his bow tie and glasses. He looks settled, as if he is married. He also looks like he doesn't get sex from his wife that often; however, Pebbles can see that he has money. Now take Will, a young, urban, 'grilled out' guy, sporting name brand gear. Although he looks hip, he is probably single, and because he is young, he does not have any money. Pebbles discerns that John will be the one who will come back every weekend. Because of this, Pebbles is going to give him something a little extra. One of the main house rules in a strip club is that you can see, but not touch, but Pebbles will make John feel special by breaking the rules. She will let him touch her on the knee, so he will keep coming back for more. Every time he comes back for more, he is going to have to give more...more money that is.

> I command your gift to resurrect!
> I command your gift to come alive!
> I command your ambition to come alive, and I bind the spirit of laziness and slothfulness!

Pebbles is building a rapport with John. After awhile, they are on a first named basis. John is full of perversion and Pebbles is full of greed. She is motivated by the dollar because she wasn't born with a silver spoon in her mouth, and she doesn't receive much support from her family. She understands that she has to do what she has to do because she is in college and she needs money to fulfill her dreams of becoming a doctor.

Do not judge Pebbles. Maybe you were not a stripper, but you were a prostitute. Anytime you sleep with somebody to pay your bills, you are a prostitute. Some of you slept with men who did not pay, and you were a stupid prostitute! If you are going to give it up, he should at least pay for half the battle. Instead, you are paying for the room, paying for the soap, paying for the tissue. The devil in hell is a liar! You need to tell that man that there is a price tag on this. If you go to hell, you might as well go rich.

Back to Pebbles and John. As I said earlier, Pebbles is full of greed and John is

# Life on Turbo

full of lust. Greed and lust are a powerful combination. She is all about the dollar while he is all about a feel. When men get to an intimate level, a chemical releases in the brain that gives them a high. Remember John is married, so you may wonder, why he is going to Pebbles when he has a 'Pebbles' at the house? Maybe because his wife (the sanctified sister) used to look like a Pebbles, now she looks more like Stone Mountain!

Unlike his wife, Pebbles will invest in John because she needs something at the end. She will work through every holiday. It might take her years, but she's going to work it out so that eventually she'll only work for three hours on a Friday and Saturday. In the process, she will make more money than the new chicken heads who work every day, and who are almost having sex with the clients. Pebbles is like Oprah. The only thing she's doing now is counseling. She's stroking John's ego. She doesn't even care about him, but she'll do what Stone Mountain won't do. Stone Mountain won't cook, but she's at church every day. Ask Stone Mountain, when was the last time she cooked for her husband and she'll stutter and sputter. Pebbles, on the other hand, will cook for John and tell him he is worthy, stroking his ego all the way.

Every man likes to be the hero. Every man has that savior mentality. Pebbles, the prophetess, knew that she was going to take 80% of John's check when she saw him a year ago. She built him up and stroked his ego, thereby, winning his loyalty and eventually his money. Now that is strategy!

## HAVE A WORK ETHIC LIKE A STRIPPER

While, I don't agree with Pebbles' lifestyle, we must examine her work ethic and motivation. Pebbles is fueled with ambition. What about you? How can you live a maximized life when you get up at 12 noon? When you don't have any money, you can't afford to sleep in.

If I tell you my family history, my age, and

what I own, you will understand what I am talking about; you'll see that I come from a place of reference. Things were not just handed to me, so do not short circuit the work that God gave me to do. He did not slap a ministry in my hands. He saw me working it. When my wife and children were asleep, I was working it. I was preaching all over and could not sleep because I did not have any money. I had to go out, get some money, and bring it home.

Today, there is no work ethic in the House of God. We have a whole bunch of saints who are stuck in the routine called life, an unfulfilling, dismal place where they were not even called to be. They are on a merry-go-round, circling around the same old thing. The bible says to press towards the mark of the prize. The high calling of God.

Are you ready? Do you understand the work ethic of Pebbles? Have you come to grips with the fact that you haven't been living life on turbo? You have been living life as a casualty. Living life carelessly on a whim, without a care in the world, but it is time to take control of the destiny God has given you. It is time to press into living life without limits and breaking glass ceilings. You are a trailblazer.

> *Many daughters have done virtuously, but thou excelleth them all.*
> *Proverbs 31:29*

This scripture may be talking about women, but there is a prophetic, profound, point God is saying in this verse. When he said 'them all,' he was referring to the boat riders, the scary scats, the jelly backs, and Mr. or Ms. Average. You know those types of people. They do not want anything more than the mediocre lives that they already lead. You have to be cutting edge, radical, relevant and revolutionary and yet refreshing. Take the superstar tennis players, Venus and Serena Williams. Whenever you hear about them playing, the sports world watches. These women are living a maximized life. What happened to the other girls? No one knows because mediocrity gets not attention.

Millionaires get paid millions to solve problems. Broke folks are poor because they run from problems. Millionaires, on the other hand, run to problems.

God is raising up people in this season who are going to surpass the enemy himself. People said you couldn't make it, but your eagle wings are spreading again. The dam is breaking in your spirit.

> *Romans 8:18 says, for I reckon that the sufferings of this present time are not worthy to be compared with the glory which shall be revealed in us. (KJV)*

*Ephesians 3:20 Now unto him that is able to do exceeding abundantly above all that we ask or think, according to the power that worketh in us (KJV)*

Your best days are still alive. So what you

messed up. Everybody has a story. You may have had a baby out of wedlock. You may have given away your virginity to someone who didn't love you. You may have been addicted in drugs, smoked black and mild, or gone to strip clubs. You may have made a bad business decision that has left you in financial ruin. God will turn your tragedies into testimonies.

## EXPERIENCE THE MAXIMIZE LIFE

There are three things that every person must do to experience the maximize life.

*2 Timothy 1:7 states For God has not given us a spirit of timidity, but of power and love and discipline. (KJV)*

### 1. You must move beyond the spirit of fear.
Fear paralyzes and causes one to be stuck. Fear will make you stay on welfare, driving a hoopty, and live in a shack. Move past fear! You cannot be afraid of what people might say about you when you get a nice car

because persecution will only affect you to the degree that you will need their approval. Fear causes people to stop at yellow lights, when you really can go through, but they will stop in fear because they may not make it. You have to move past the opinion of men. You have to be interested in what God says. You have to be in love with your destiny, and the gift of God on the inside of you. In order to do that, you must move beyond fear.

**2. Not only does fear paralyze, but it also prophesy's.** You can be in fear so much that it will begin to prophesy to your destiny. Fear will say that your mama didn't make it, so you won't make it. You may be married to a preacher and he might go around the world, yet you stay behind dictated by the voice of fear. Fear will become your prophetic puppet master. With a tug on the invisible strings, it will tell you how far you can go, and how long you can last. The enemy doesn't care who you are connected to, he's after you. It is time to shake the puppet master of fear off. It is time to move past the mundane. It is time to move past mediocrity. It is time to move past the same old same old. It is time to get off the boat!

**3. Move beyond the spirit of failure.** You may have made bad decisions, financial moves or business plans. You may have experienced a bad marriage or bad relationships. I am sorry that happened to you, but you have to move beyond yesterday's pain. I am sorry it did not work out and you lost some money. You had your share of difficulties. You had your share of problems, and you are not your mistake. This year, you are moving past your failure. You are going higher in God. You are growing stronger and going to a deeper level in him.

### WE'VE ALL BEEN THERE BEFORE

I'd like to share a personal story about me moving beyond fear and failure. When I was younger, around the time that I had just come to the Lord, I was on my way to cash a paycheck at a bank. I went inside the bank, cashed my check and was on my way to preach a revival in Savannah, GA when a man with a foreign accent approached me and said, he needed to talk to me. I didn't understand what was going on around me, but when the encounter ended, he ended up taking all my money without putting a gun to my head. He didn't hold me up, he just took it because he told me that I would get more money if I loaned him all of my money. This is one of the biggest scams out there. As it turned out, I didn't receive anything. They stole my money because I made a bad decision.

We make bad decisions in marriage. God said from death do we part, for better or worse, in sickness and in health. Yet, that person may have put you through hell. You may have thought that he loved you. You know you should have listened to your parents when they told you not to marry him. Despite that, it is time to move past the spirit of failure. Refuse to allow the spirit of failure to hold your future hostage.

In 1 Corinthians 15:9. Paul moved beyond the pain and failure of yesterday and stepped into his destiny.

## ARE YOU READY?

You are not the only one who has experienced failure. We all have at some point in our lives. Like Apostle Paul, you are what you are and by the grace of God, he

> *I am the least of the apostles, that I am not meet to be called an apostle because I persecuted the church of God. But by the grace of God, I am what I am: His grace which was bestowed upon me was not in vain. 1 Cor. 15-9*

turned your failure into focus! You are more observant, more watchful than before. The devil will not catch you twice. You have more wisdom!

This year, you are not going to give into flesh, fear or failure. You may have had moments of insanity. You may have felt like sitting down and dying like the prophet Elijah, but you can't die, be depressed, or give up. There is no give up in you! Those days are over! You are getting ready to move into a maximized life in Christ. You are going to have an agenda. Whatever you do in this season, you are going to schedule it because you realize that your life is purposeful. It has meaning. You have yourself some business. You have destiny. Not everyone is qualified to be on your schedule. Those people, who used to occupy your time, may have had your problem, they may have had your demons and shared in your weaknesses, but you have just hooked up with someone who has your answer. You are a champion and you have power!

I was watching a segment about a family of wild dogs on the National Geographic channel. A mother and her pack of little wild puppies lived in the tall grass of the savannah. The mother was leading her babies across the road. As she was about to step out, she was careful to look from side to side before allowing them to cross. When she thought their passage was safe, she started to cross. All of the puppies began to follow suit when out of nowhere a truck came barreling over the hill, slamming into the mother. She immediately dropped down on the side of the road, and closed her eyes. Thinking she was dead, the man stopped the truck and walked over to move her body. What he could not see was the glimmer in her eye as she remembered what she had given birth to weeks earlier. Her babies were waiting for her! She had started something, and had to finish. Out of nowhere, she sprang to her feet, and shot across the road with her puppies in tow.

That sounded like you, didn't it? Suddenly, tragedy, suffering, and anguish hit your life overnight, and the enemy left you for dead. He thought your dream had died. He thought your passion and purpose died, but it is not over until God says so. It is not over until you get the victory, until God gives you a song and a dance. Until you walk in power, it is not over! Like that mother dog, you have to jump up and fulfill your assignment!

Are you ready for this year? Are you ready to birth out that dream? Are you all set to cross over into being the person who God created you to be, and live the way He desires for you to live? Then buckle up because you are traveling full speed ahead this year. Get ready! Life as you know it will never be the same. On your mark...get set...GO!

www.ingramcontent.com/pod-product-compliance
Lightning Source LLC
Chambersburg PA
CBHW070651300426
44111CB00013B/2363